T0199128

The TREE TOP, the Wind, and the BALLOON

STORY and ILLUSTRATIONS bY:
MARY CATHERINE RISHCOFF

To order additional copies of this book, contact:
Xlibris
1-888-795-4274
www.Xlibris.com
Orders@Xlibris.com

I
dedicate
the following
book
to the
City of Allentown,
Pennsylvania, U.S.A.
where
I
learned
to play.

When I lived on the east side of the City of Allentown, there were two parks nearby my home. I played often in the park named Keck Park, including drawing. The City of Allentown police were always available to me whenever I needed a friendly face, as were the park-goers. Thanks ever so much to all these people for their warmth and friendships.

I saw that the treetop reached very, very high. It stood very tall. The color of the foliage was green.

Then, a zephyr rustled through the treetop. The greens shifted.

Suddenly, up, up rose a single balloon. It was bright red in color.

Higher and higher, the balloon climbed. A blue-colored ribbon dangled at the bottom of the balloon. At first sight, I thought it a kite.

Again the wind moved. The greens seemed to volley as the balloon continued to rise. The balloon was quite small in comparison to the treetop.

The breeze blew both the treetop and the balloon ever so gently.

The wind flew the balloon far, far away.

The wind continued to blow softly. So too, the balloon continued to climb slowly. The foliage of the treetop pressed eastward, as if chasing the balloon.

Away, away departed the balloon. It disappeared from view, Ribbon and all.

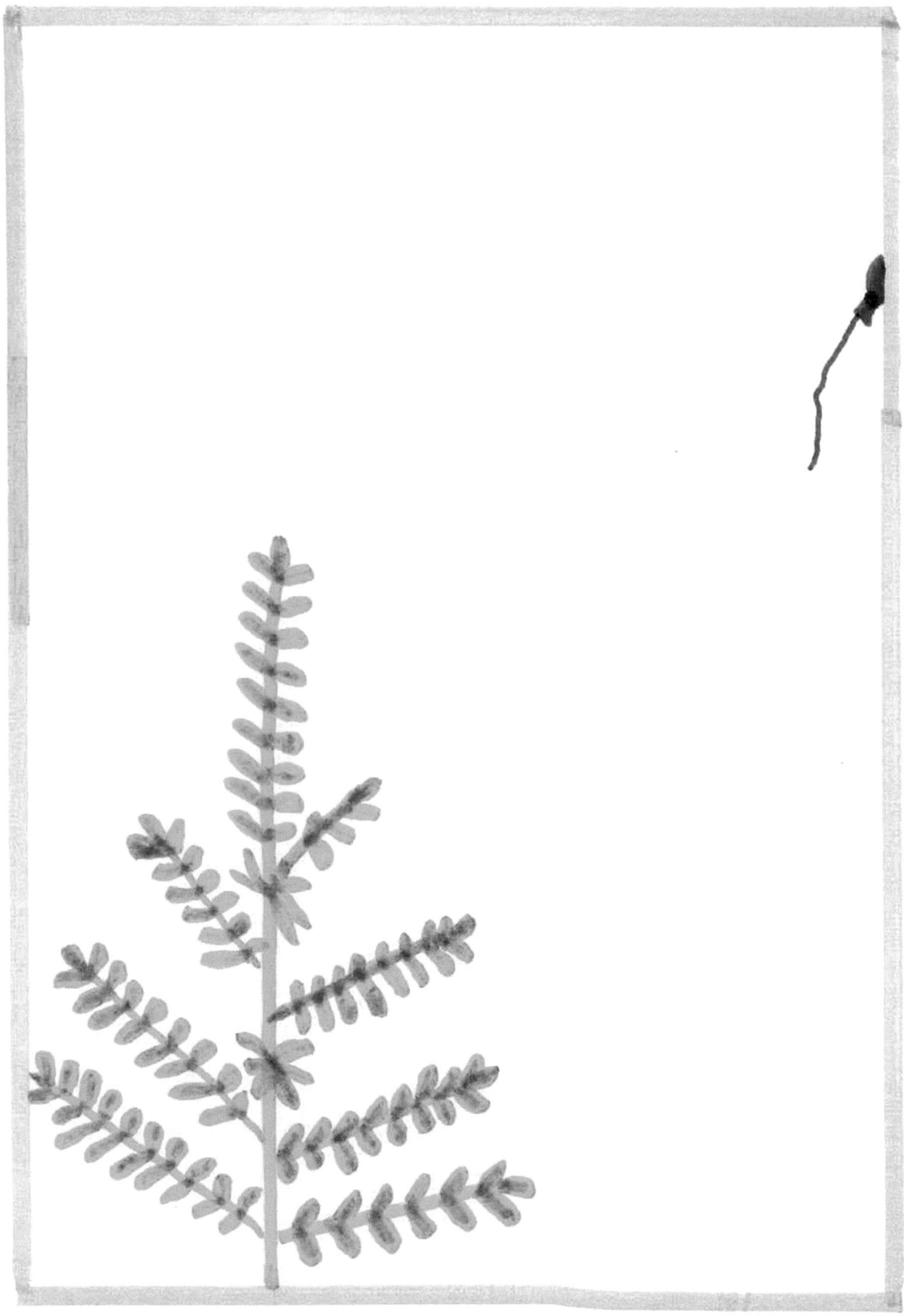

The wind waned. The treetop stood alone. The tree was named, "The Hyperion Tree", a coast redwood growing in Redwood National Park, California, U.S.A..

THE

END

rinted in the United States
y Bookmasters